I0150451

AS SEEN ON
Oprah's OWN Network
Super Soul Sunday

7 PATHS
to Healing Your Relationship

THE
WISDOM TRIANGLE
WORKBOOK

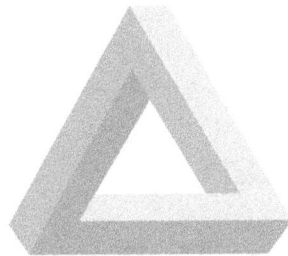

ROCHELLE L. COOK
MA., CHT.

Copyright © 2016 by Rochelle L. Cook MA., ChT.
All rights reserved. No part of this publication may be reproduced, distributed, or transmitted in any form or by any means, including photocopying, recording, or other electronic or mechanical methods, without the prior written permission of the publisher, except in the case of brief quotations embodied in critical reviews and certain other noncommercial uses permitted by copyright law.

For permission requests, write to the publisher, addressed "Attention: Permissions Coordinator," at the address below.
Bloom Factor Press
4115 Glencoe Avenue, Suite 105
Marina del Rey, CA 90292
www.BloomFactorPress.com

Ordering Information:
Quantity sales. Special expanded wholesale availability is available on quantity purchases by corporations, associations, and others. For details, contact the publisher CreateSpace >>> www.createspace.com/pub/l/createspacedirect.do or order it through one of the regular wholesalers, e.g., Ingram.

ISBN-10 0-9891931-3-6
ISBN-13: 978-0-9891931-3-9

Library of Congress In-Publication Data
Cook MA., ChT. Rochelle L.
7 Paths to Healing Your Relationship – The Workbook!
1. Spirituality 2. Psychology 3 Self Help

Project, cover and book design directed by Michael Glock Ph.D.
Typesetting by Ramesh Kumar Pitchai
Interior typeset in Sabon (body) & Oswald (Chapter)
Front/back cover painting by © Gregg Chadwick Used by permission: May 10 2016
www.greggchadwick.com/
Printed in the United States of America
First printing – September 2016

20 19 18 17 16 15 14 13 12 11 10 9 8 7 6 5 4 3 2

DEDICATION DATE:

....

I ....

Dedicate the work in this book to

....

....

....

....

....

....

....

....

....

....

....

....

....

....

N.B. Dedicate this page to yourself or to a significant person. Show them this journal a few years after you have filled it up and tell them your story.

Disclaimer

This workbook is not intended as a substitute for the medical advice of physicians or mental license professionals. The reader should regularly consult a physician in matters relating to his/her health, mental health and particularly with respect to any psychological or physical symptoms that may require diagnosis or medical attention.

CONTENTS

Early Acclaim ix

Introduction III –
Wisdom Triangle Book by Rochelle L. Cook MA., ChT. 1

1   Exercise 1 – The Story Book Syndrome 9
2   Exercise 2 – Chaos as Catalyst 23
3   Exercise 3 – Path One – Denial 33
4   Exercise 4 – Path Two – Settling 49
5   Exercise 5 – Path Three – Playing Out 69
6   Exercise 6 – Path Four – Acceptance 85
7   Exercise 7 – Path Five – Intention 101
8   Exercise 8 – Path Six – Spirituality 113
9   Exercise 9 – Path Seven – The New Story 125
10   Exercise 10 – Reflections on Parenting 141
11   Exercise 11 – Conclusion 155

A Tree Says: My Strength is Trust. 165
Notes 171

EARLY ACCLAIM FOR

7 Paths To Healing Your Relationship - The Wisdom Triangle Workbook

Wow! What can I say other than Rochelle is one of the most amazingly authentic people on the planet. Even when walking through some of my darkest moments I never felt judgment or discomfort when I am doing work with her. I have seen a lot of people for therapy and other inner work-they all pale in comparison to the work that Rochelle naturally does. I HIGHLY recommend Rochelle if you have blocks or if you suffer from anything mentally, spiritually or physically, as she is a true miracle worker! I will always utilize her services as she makes me feel beyond good during and after our sessions!!

Amy F. Seattle, WA

Rochelle is an inspiring and intelligent person. She has helped me so quickly with so many deep rooted issues that I feel like I have been stuck with for so long. I cannot thank her enough for helping me start a new journey. Her technique works, and it is a wonderful to be in her company.

I have never tried hypnotherapy before, but I am so grateful to have found Rochelle because I have realized that is she gives so much more. She is an incredible spiritual guide, filled with light and love.

India W. Venice, CA

I strongly recommend Rochelle as a therapist. I went in to see Rochelle based on a good recommendation by a friend because I was dealing with difficult family relationships stemming from the recent passing of a parent. I gained so much from her incredibly accurate and helpful analysis, and she provides a number of powerful visualization and spiritual exercises that helped me gain a better and healthier perception of others and myself. I feel as though a great weight has been lifted off my shoulders and I look forward to continued work with such a great professional.

Tim C. Venice, CA

Rochelle gets five stars because she is DEDICATED TO HELPING OTHERS & she has the SKILL SET TO DO IT. Her experience, training, intuitive nature & compassion helped me connect with my past and guided me through a TRANSFORMATIONAL PROCESS that gave me understanding and freedom. I HIGHLY RECOMMEND you to meet with Rochelle and experience this for yourself. Thank you Rochelle for all you have given me so far.

Maxine W. Los Angeles, CA

Rochelle is the real deal! She is extremely articulate, smart, honest and warm. She gained my trust almost instantaneously, she is incredible. Ask for what you want and you shall receive with this miracle worker. She has changed my life and I've only had 4 sessions.

Annie P. Manhattan, NY

Transformational is an apt description of the experience derived from Rochelle's expertise. With her intuitive, intelligent and enthusiastic approach to hypnosis, she brought an astonishing amount of clarity and peace in our sessions. She is a warm, spiritual and sensitive person and a brilliant communicator. I immediately felt comfortable with her and confident in her abilities. The process is fascinating, enjoyable and very effective. I highly recommend Rochelle to anyone grappling with the many issues she is dedicated to healing.

Michele P. Beverly Hills, CA

Introduction

7 Paths to Healing your Relationship
The Wisdom Triangle Workbook

By Rochelle L. Cook MA., ChT.

"You can search throughout the entire universe for someone who is more deserving of your love and affection than you are yourself, and that person is not to be found anywhere. You yourself, as much as anybody in the entire universe deserves your love and affection." ~ Buddha

Before you use this workbook please read the book, *The Soul's Coach 7 Paths to Healing Your Relationship.* By reading the book and understanding it's 7 paths you will effectively work the questions outlined in the text below. Please take your time, Rome wasn't built in a day, **be honest with yourself,** and allow your heart, spirit and mind to heal.

INSTRUCTIONS:

The workbook comprises of twelve exercises and we suggest you do four exercises per month, that's one a week for three months. Our experience with clients has shown us that taking three months from start-to-finish produces long-lasting results. At the completion of each exercise you have a short wisdom triangle section. This allows you to recap the exercise in a condensed manner, refer to these pages often for the years to come.

THE WISDOM TRIANGLE?

The Wisdom Triangle is an impossible figure, a type of optical illusion that flows along "infinitely." It consists of a two-dimensional figure, which is instantly and subconsciously interpreted by the visual system as representing a projection of a three-dimensional object.

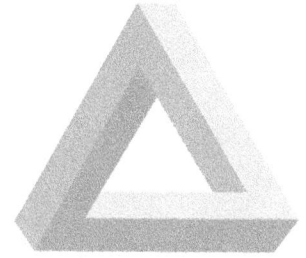

We all collect knowledge that we convert into wisdom throughout our lifetime. Wisdom creates the chapters in our lives that one day become our legacy and our own "wise" storybook. Knowledge and its companion, wisdom are the empowering engines that produce you, yet, the more we learn, the more we don't know.

Sometimes wisdom is found where we least expect it. Through good times and bad, through the beautiful flower you walk by every day, waiting for you to just "stop" look and be present while admiring its beauty. Life's ups and downs contain wisdom; from interacting with our grandparents, professors, philosophers and the mundane everyday life that is full of opportunity, to retreats, mindfulness practices and literature and workbooks.

We have been taught that some things are forbidden, however it is important to do things that are outside of your comfort zone, or like Eve, eat the forbidden fruit. Perhaps for Eve, eating the apple was a mistake, but it was critical for her evolution. Living in paradise is a false illusion; it is the storybook syndrome! We have to learn to navigate the stormy seas and experience the hurricanes and beautiful calm sunsets of everything we encounter in life. You cannot appreciate the good things in life unless you have experienced the opposites.

By using the wisdom triangle you will learn to appreciate the "wrong" lessons. You will learn to accept the "wrong" and make it ok, it's just a lesson.

The wisdom triangle is you, and all of it makes sense. It is made of three parts. **Your past;** is and has a flat quality; what do you believe, what happened to shape your memory of your storybook syndrome? **The here and now;** what are your thoughts and behavior trying to tell you? This is the power of being in the now! Ultimately this leads to your **"truth"** your new story and unfolds from the work. You become the "new story" that contains all the lessons you have learned, the insights you have gained and the collected wisdom you have chosen to embrace – all this continues to flow infinitely, moving and shaping your experiences.

By learning and practicing The Wisdom Triangle, by questioning your thoughts and actions, you will better understand life's lessons; you will uncover the meaning behind your engagement with the world and your suffering. Some of us are privileged to be able to change the way we think, we control our thoughts, which shape our daily lives. Are you one of them? What would happen if you embraced this idea and lived your life; committing yourself to doing the work in a fiduciary manner?

According to the Merriam Webster's dictionary the simple definition of INFINITE means, having no limits, and extremely large or great.

What would happen if you embraced this idea of having no limits and lived extremely large or great? Would you pledge to question, learn and select how you choose to participate without judgment in your world? I can assure you of this, if you are willing to read and work the questions and follow the guidelines in this workbook – you will notice a new and profound mindfulness emerging, your thoughts shifting into positive directions, your whole-life changing. You will blossom and bloom and be the juicy-fruit that attracts and nourishes.

REALITY IS PERCEPTION:

The Soul's Coach – 7 Paths to Healing Relationship Workbook will show you how your own reality is a reflection of your own perceptions. Whatever is going on "out there" is a mirror that holds the key to your healing. By looking into the mirror and honestly seeing the refection of yourself in it, only then, will you be able to begin changing. By going through the *7 Paths to Healing Relationships – The Wisdom Triangle Workbook*, you will realize *how your life has and continues to show up is the outcome of your thoughts* and that *changing your thinking will change your life.*

You will be travelling on 7 different paths while you journey through the workbook answering the specific questions. You will likely encounter old memories that surface from the depths, or remember traumatic incidents that you have buried and abandoned. You will likely remember what you have forgotten and become much more aware of synchronistic events, blessings and gratitude's along the way.

The 7 paths you will be journeying along will be: **Denial:** we live our lives oblivious to the reality of our situation. **Settling:** we feel unworthy or undeserving so we take what we can get. **Playing Out:** the unhealthy behaviors we unconsciously exhibit offer hints as to what in us needs to be healed. **Acceptance:** we recognize that we need to change, and understand our trauma as a stage on the journey of transformation. **Intention:** we begin to act from a conscious, sensible mind; we "set our sails" toward the life of our dreams. **Spirituality:** we live in the awareness that our thoughts, words and actions matter; we matter; love & peace are possible. **The New Story:** to write our new story, first we have to identify and heal the old one.

On the *7 Paths to Healing your Relationship – The Wisdom Triangle Workbook*, you will see how you will embark on the work from different arrival and destinations – "ports." There are those who have been meditating for years, but have not dealt with their emotional childhood crisis. There are those who can identify their trigger in a current situation and understand its source, but are unable to move forward into acceptance or commit to intentions that will turn their lives around. It is not a map to be followed step by step in order to reach the destination. It must not be understood as a linear process starting with Denial and followed progressively to the endpoint. It is rather a free, creative process that shapes itself differently for each one, and for some it *will be* a map to be followed with precision and exactness. ***You can do any exercise in any order as long as you do four exercises per month and allow yourself three months to complete your circuit.***

The workbook is designed to help you understand in a step-by-step manner how to reframe your perceptions so that you can finally change the way you think. You may notice that some of the exercises and its contents are repetitive, this is more than ok – it has been designed like this. The more you read, and hear your own words and story in your own mind, and mentally "see" your own perceptions – your new story will begin to emerge. You will advance, become more active and energetic because a new direction and future will be emerging. Through the repetitions and the insights gained using the workbook, new habits will form, new thinking will flourish, bloom and prevail.

Working through this workbook slowly and taking your time is key to developing your new thought pattern. Do not rush through the process! Take the three months as prescribed! Think deeply and only work on one exercise at a time. Give yourself time to reflect and practice what you have learned. If at any time you feel the need for extra assistance, reach out and seek professional guidance. Remember, none of us are perfect, change takes time, Rome was not built in a day.

"Healing is a mystery, a dance between you, this workbook, your counselor, and especially the Great Spirit. So stay open and alert, and tune in so you can hear the guidance from within and without. This is an adventure of a lifetime in body and soul." ~ Rochelle L. Cook

"The life of every man is a diary in which he means to write one story, and writes another; and his humblest hour is when he compares the volume as it is with what he vowed to make it." ~ J. M. Barrie

REMEMBER – WE RECOMMEND YOU ALSO KEEP A GUIDING JOURNAL!

This is a workbook that goes hand-in-hand with the book, *The Soul's Coach – 7 Paths to Healing Your Relationship*. It has been designed as a specific practice to support a detailed inquiry, however we also suggest that you also journal.

Journaling on a daily basis is the most powerful cornerstone and habit you can acquire. If done correctly, you will show up better in every area of your life. Without question, journaling has always been the number one factor to everything I've done, including my husband and daughter, well in my life. This includes the lives of my clients.

By writing in your journal in the morning or evening, you will quickly see the incongruences in your life. Some people write in the morning and the evening, this creates a safe container that allows one to stay on course. You will see clearly what negative thoughts need to be removed and what positive and reframed thoughts should be included in your life. Along with the workbook, journaling is a wonderful and powerful facilitator to self-discovery. Through my own journaling I've come to form my sense of identity and path in life.

You will notice that at the end of each exercise in this workbook and in the journal we ask you to write what you are forgiving yourself for and what you are grateful for. We do this so that each day you will clearly speak to the universe and thereby change your perception.

Science has proven that the practice of gratitude is a way to overcome several psychological challenges. The benefits are endless, here a few to think about:

- Gratitude makes you more happy
- Gratitude strengthens your emotions
- Gratitude increases spirituality
- Gratitude makes you healthier
- Gratitude makes you more optimistic
- Gratitude lets you live longer
- Gratitude helps you bounce back from challenges

NOW LETS GET TO WORK!

EXERCISE 1 - THE STORY BOOK SYNDROME

"Healing is a matter of time,
but it is sometimes also a matter of opportunity." ~ Hippocrates

We don't have to live and be what we were taught!
~ Rochelle L. Cook MA., ChT.

In one way or another, at some point in our lives, we all suffer from what I call the Story Book Syndrome. From classical literature to popular media we are told enchanting stories about knights carrying their princesses off into the sunset. Such perfection as displayed in the Story Book does not exist and only creates false expectations. No relationship is perfect. Every relationship requires work and this work starts with work on ourselves.

Carefully read the questions that follow, meditate on them, allow any images or thoughts to surface and then write down what emerges in the following blank pages. Allow yourself to be inspired and surprised by what manifests.

1. What was one of your favorite stories as a child?

2. What did this story teach you and your inner-child? Based on this story, how have you been living your life?

....

....

....

....

....

....

....

....

....

....

....

....

....

....

....

....

....

....

....

....

....

3. What was/is your Story Book Syndrome? What were YOU taught? Include information from your family, significant others, culture, community, work, religion, films and the media?

4. Where did the illusion of the Story Book Syndrome lead you?

5. Life is a Seesaw, what does your life look like when everything is going well, what does it look like when things are going wrong? To refresh yourself on the, "Seesaw" please refer to chapter one, in *The Soul's Coach – 7 Paths to Healing Your Relationship*

6. What would it look like if you sat in the middle of the seesaw and remained neutral? What if right or wrong did not exist? How would you feel? What would you do? The middle is neutral, this is where we accept that life goes up and down and make it ok.

7. Write a letter to yourself, what do you want to say about what you were taught to believe? Write the letter to the part of you that hurts, or is confused. You can also write to your inner-child. What did he or she take on as the, "way it should be?" Example: Dear Self or inner-child, I am sorry that for so long you have had to buy into the misbelief that if ...... (Continue)

THE WISDOM TRIANGLE

This is a recap that you can always return to and remind yourself of the TRUTH of your situation. Be specific to the exercise you just completed. Just write down 1 or 2 sentences, keep it simple. If necessary remember that you are talking to your inner-child. What does he or she need to finally understand?

1. <u>The past:</u> (What happened?) Example: I learned that I am unworthy of love because I was not wanted.

....

....

....

....

2. <u>The here and now:</u> (What story or behavior was playing out or is playing out that you are understanding and letting go of?) Example: I want to be loved and approved of so badly that I chase love away, or, I wanted to be loved and approved of so badly that at the time I chased love away. I still fear I will be alone because I'm not good enough to be loved.

....

....

....

....

3. <u>The "TRUTH": Example:</u> (What is the real healthy TRUTH about your situation?) My old storybook syndrome is not true! I have always been worthy of love by just being me. It does not matter what they think, it matters what "I think." I am a good person that anyone would be lucky to have in his or her lives!

....

....

....

Write 7 reasons why you forgive yourself. *Example: I forgive myself for buying into the misbelief that I have to do what I was taught. I forgive myself for the misbelief that if I do not live in "my" storybook that I am WRONG. I forgive myself for the misbelief that I am bad because I did not live up to my family's expectations. BE AS SPECIFIC AS YOU CAN.*

1. I forgive myself for the misbelief that, and the truth is:

....

....

2. I forgive myself for the misbelief that, and the truth is:

....

....

3. I forgive myself for the misbelief that, and the truth is:

....

....

4. I forgive myself for the misbelief that, and the truth is:

....

....

5. I forgive myself for the misbelief that, and the truth is:

....

....

6. I forgive myself for the misbelief that, and the truth is:

....

....

7. I forgive myself for the misbelief that, and the truth is:

....

....

Now write 7 reasons why you are grateful. Example. I am grateful that I lived in the storybook because I now know what I do not want to experience. I am grateful that I understand my storybook syndrome because now I know what I want to experience. I am grateful because I know that I only have to win my own approval not my family. I am grateful to be alive!

1. I am grateful for, and the truth is:

....

....

2. I am grateful for, and the truth is:

....

....

3. I am grateful for, and the truth is:

....

....

4. I am grateful for, and the truth is:

....

....

5. I am grateful for, and the truth is:

....

....

6. I am grateful for, and the truth is:

....

....

7. I am grateful for, and the truth is:

....

....

EXERCISE 2 - CHAOS AS CATALYST

Through life's circumstances our world becomes chaotic yet we feel comfortable in it. We live in what we know.

~ Rochelle L. Cook MA., ChT.

Our basic identity is formed in childhood and as adults we are still only grown up children reacting automatically and unconsciously to life's ups and downs. We unconsciously create the chaos we live in and this chaos becomes our comfort zone. Most of us refuse to recognize it as chaos, even when it stares us in the face.

Carefully read the questions that follow, meditate on them, allow any images or thoughts to surface and then write down what emerges in the following blank pages. Allow yourself to be inspired and surprised by what manifests.

1. **What chaos are you experiencing in your life? Think of a tornado that is out of control, what does it look like?**

....

....

....

....

....

....

....

....

....

....

....

....

....

....

....

....

....

....

....

....

....

2. How do you feel when you are in the middle of your tornado?

3. What is the root cause of this chaos? "I am creating this chaotic way of living because I am used to..." Where did you learn about, "your chaos?"

4. How would your life be if you turned your chaos into harmony? How would feel?

5. The Scars of Trauma, what are the scars? How do you feel? How are you protecting yourself? Why? If the, "scar could talk what would it have to say?" Example: I have to protect myself because I? ……. (Continue)

THE WISDOM TRIANGLE

This is a recap that you can always return to and remind yourself of the TRUTH of your situation. Be specific to the exercise you just completed. Just write down 1 or 2 sentences, keep it simple. If necessary remember that you are talking to your inner-child. What does he or she need to finally understand?

1. <u>The past:</u> (What happened?) Example: I learned that I am unworthy of love because I was not wanted.

....

....

....

....

....

2. <u>The here and now:</u> (What chaos is playing out in your life?) Example: I live in fear that "they" may abandon me! I chase love away.

....

....

....

....

....

3. <u>The "TRUTH": Example:</u> (What is the real healthy TRUTH about your situation?) I know longer have to create chaos in my life. My past is not my here and now. My life is calm and peaceful, the past and its chaos are gone.

....

....

....

....

....

Write 7 reasons why you forgive yourself. Example: I forgive myself for buying into the misbelief that I have to live in chaos, I no longer allow the past to contaminate my future. BE AS SPECIFIC AS YOU CAN.

1. I forgive myself for the misbelief that, and the truth is:

....

....

2. I forgive myself for the misbelief that, and the truth is:

....

....

3. I forgive myself for the misbelief that, and the truth is:

....

....

4. I forgive myself for the misbelief that, and the truth is:

....

....

5. I forgive myself for the misbelief that, and the truth is:

....

....

6. I forgive myself for the misbelief that, and the truth is:

....

....

7. I forgive myself for the misbelief that, and the truth is:

....

***Now write 7 reasons why you are grateful.** Example. I am grateful for the lessons I have learned. I am a good, worthy and loving person.*

1. I am grateful for, and the truth is:

....

....

2. I am grateful for, and the truth is:

....

....

3. I am grateful for, and the truth is:

....

....

4. I am grateful for, and the truth is:

....

....

5. I am grateful for, and the truth is:

....

....

6. I am grateful for, and the truth is:

....

....

7. I am grateful for, and the truth is:

....

....

EXERCISE 3 - PATH ONE - DENIAL

If we deny our problems we don't have to face the music.
~ Rochelle L. Cook MA., ChT.

Living in denial allows us to avoid confronting our challenge, a challenge that could lead to a breakthrough. When bad things happen to us we are upset, traumatized, the rug has been pulled from underneath our feet, yet we look the other way, too afraid to face the situation. The only way out of this conundrum is to recognize what triggered it, ride the energy back to a similar experience in our childhood that is the root cause of the present upset – and resolve that.

Are you Present? Relationships are often compromised because we are obsessed with the past and all of the traumatic experiences we have endured; we are convinced that our future will be doomed as well. We take our past, we project it into our future, and make it our here and now.

> *"Clearly, all fear has an element of resistance and a leaning away from the moment. Its dynamic is not unlike that of strong desire except that fear leans backward into the last safe moment while desire leans forward toward the next possibility of satisfaction. Each lacks presence."*
>
> ~ *Stephen Levine*

Carefully read the questions that follow, meditate on them, allow any images or thoughts to surface and then write down what emerges in the following blank pages. Allow yourself to be inspired and surprised by what manifests.

1. What are you afraid of now. in the present?

2. If you remain in denial, what "won't" happen?

3. Is this true that your past will repeat itself in the future? Think carefully before you answer this question.

4. What is the TRUTH?

THE ENDLESS RUN

The Endless Run, we spend our lives running because the moment we stop we feel how miserable we are. If we run fast enough our skeletons in our closet wont get us.

1. <u>What are you running away from?</u>

....
....
....
....
....

2. <u>What will happen if you stop running?</u>

....
....
....
....
....

3. <u>Where did you learn that running would save you?</u>

....
....
....
....
....

4. <u>Is this true?</u>

....

....

....

....

....

5. <u>What is the TRUTH?</u>

....

....

....

....

....

WHY DO WE LOOK THE OTHER WAY?

It is a known fact that we will endure almost anything rather than change. Change is difficult.

1. <u>What are you afraid to change?</u>

....

....

....

....

....

2. <u>What would happen if you did change?</u>

....

....

....

3. **Write both the negative and the POSITIVE, would the positive be a better scenario? Why?**

4. **Are you willing to change your thinking?**

RECOGNIZE YOUR TRIGGERS

We call "a trigger" something or someone that upsets you that throws you off your horse, as we say. Back in your past there was an incident or event, small or large, that included words, actions, sights, smells and sounds that caused you deep upset, even trauma, and to this day when even a hint of a reminder of any of those elements is present, you react dramatically, unconsciously, and you may even experience a similar trauma – you have just been triggered!

"Identifying triggers is the first step out of denial. Work to conquer the belief behind the trigger, release the emotional charge you still carry as a result, and get on with your wonderful happy life!"

1. When was the last time you were triggered?

....

....

....

....

2. What triggered you and why?

....

....

....

....

3. How did you react?

....

....

....

....

4. Thinking back, what is the truth? Example: I was triggered because.......

....

....

....

....

5. How can you reframe the trigger, the upset, into the positive, the truth? (What can you say to yourself that will allow you to calm yourself and feel safe?)

....

....

....

....

....

FEAR AND UNCERTAINTY

Fear gets in the way of everything. If you are like me, I can only imagine how many times you wanted to make a decision of some sort and fear stopped you. What I discovered is that fear is nothing but "chatter." It is made up of all the negative projections we have absorbed from everyone and everything around us through our lives.

1. What are you denying – what don't you want to look at and why?

....

....

....

....

....

2. What kind of behaviors have your denial led you to? Is there a pattern that keeps playing out?

....

....

....

....

....

3. How would your life be if you faced that which you are denying?

....

....

....

....

....

4. Where did you learn this fear?

....

....

....

....

....

5. What is the "real" TRUTH?

....

....

....

....

....

....

....

....

....

....

....

THE WISDOM TRIANGLE

This is a recap that you can always return to and remind yourself of the TRUTH of your situation. Be specific to the exercise you just completed. Just write down 1 or 2 sentences, keep it simple. If necessary remember that you are talking to your inner-child. What does he or she need to finally understand?

1. <u>The past:</u> (What happened?) *Example: I lived in an abusive relationship but did not recognize what I was in.*

....
....
....
....
....

2. <u>The here and now:</u> (What behavior was playing out or is playing out that you are understanding and letting go of?) *Example: What have you been denying? I allowed myself to be abused, I did not respect myself by saying no. I lived in my fantasy looking through rose colored glasses.*

....
....
....
....
....

3. <u>The "TRUTH":</u> *Example: (What is the real healthy TRUTH about your situation?) I deserve love, denial is only stopping me from finding love and peace.*

....
....
....
....

Write 7 reasons why you forgive yourself.

1. I forgive myself for the misbelief that, and the truth is:

....

....

2. I forgive myself for the misbelief that, and the truth is:

....

....

3. I forgive myself for the misbelief that, and the truth is:

....

....

4. I forgive myself for the misbelief that, and the truth is:

....

....

5. I forgive myself for the misbelief that, and the truth is:

....

....

6. I forgive myself for the misbelief that, and the truth is:

....

....

7. I forgive myself for the misbelief that, and the truth is:

....

....

Now write 7 reasons why you are grateful.

1. I am grateful for, and the truth is:

....

....

2. I am grateful for, and the truth is:

....

....

3. I am grateful for, and the truth is:

....

....

4. I am grateful for, and the truth is:

....

....

5. I am grateful for, and the truth is:

....

....

6. I am grateful for, and the truth is:

....

....

7. I am grateful for, and the truth is:

....

....

EXERCISE 4 - PATH TWO - SETTLING

I Am Not Good Enough for a Better Relationship, so I'll Settle for This One, Even Though I Am Not Happy in It.

We settle into an unhealthy and unhappy relationship because leaving it is too frightening, we'd be pitted against an unknown future that could be even worse. So we take what we can get and hold on to damaging situations. If we track this pattern back to an earlier time in our lives, we'll discover that somewhere in our formative years we experienced pain and trauma from which we concluded that we were unworthy and undeserving of a better life. That conclusion is ingrained in our subconscious and still calling the shots. But with inner-child work and by identifying our projections it is possible to mend the wounds of the past, to recognize our worth, and find the strength of heart to move forward toward the life and relationship we seek.

The Inner-child Our inner-child is creative, imaginative, adorable and innocent. Unfortunately, it is also the part in us that was hurt in childhood, and the wounds are still bleeding. Until we heal this part, we are all children living in an adult body. Our inner-child is unconsciously running our adult behaviors and reactions.

"The most sophisticated people I know - inside they are all children." ~ Jim Henson

Carefully read the questions that follow, meditate on them, allow any images or thoughts to surface and then write down what emerges in the following blank pages. Allow yourself to be inspired and surprised by what manifests.

1. If the child could speak, what would he or she say? Example, I am upset because I? Please, allow the inner-child to speak, take your time and write as long as you need to. If necessary, use more paper. I even recommend that your inner-child use his or her favorite color of ink. Children love to color and it allows them to express themselves better. Drawing pictures is good too.

2. How would the inner-child respond to; I would really like it if?

3. List all the ways your inner-child is creative, adorable, and innocent.

4. Now, it is your turn as the adult, re-parenting your own inner-child to write back. What do you want to say to them that will answer their questions and allow them to feel safe?

....

....

....

....

....

....

....

....

....

....

....

....

....

....

....

....

....

....

....

....

....

....

....

....

Recognize Your Inner-child Triggers. Look at what upsets and causes you to react in a negative way. It is usually something carried into adulthood from the past.

"Pretty much all the honest truth telling there is in the world is done by children."
~ *Oliver Wendell Holmes, author and poet*

1. **Can you locate one or two disturbing incidents in time and place?**

....
....
....
....
....

2. What was your experience as a child that is begging to this day to be heard, understood and healed?

....
....
....
....
....

3. What conclusions and decisions have you derived from your traumatic childhood experiences about the world and about yourself?

....
....
....
....
....

4. What is the TRUTH?

....

....

....

....

....

Listen to and Parent Your Inner-Child. Our inner-child desperately wants to be approved of and loved.

Assure the inner-child that it will never be invalidated; give it what he/or she was deprived of, tell this precious being I love you.

1. Write a letter to the inner-child assuring he or she that you will promise to protect, love, approve and honor their path. What can you write that the child needs to hear?

....

....

....

....

....

....

....

....

....

....

....

....

....

The Voice of Abandonment We've all experienced being bombarded by unstoppable negative thoughts all day and night long. This negative chatter gets in the way of our healthy and creative thoughts, and opens the door to an avalanche of fearful beliefs, feelings and behaviors. When you hear these negative thoughts – the voice of your inner-child – listen, acknowledge its pain and fear, speak to it calmly and lovingly, and free your inner-child and yourself from the endless slavery of unhealed childhood trauma.

1. You have just written a letter to your inner-child. What can you tell your child about his or her scary thoughts? Remind he or she where those thoughts come from.

....

....

....

....

....

2. What is the TRUTH?

....

....

....

....

....

3. What is their new reality?

....

....

....

....

....

Why Settle?

It's time to take care of yourself! Animals go into a quiet corner and lick their wounds, nurturing themselves. Having realized that you are settling for a life or a relationship that is "less than" what you want or deserve, you may want to take a step back and search for the lesson you are being asked to face. Be kind to yourself.

1. Again, ask yourself, what does the inner-child has to tell you?

2. Where did you learn that settling is okay?

3. When did you begin to think: "I am not good enough for a healthy relationship, so I'll just settle for this one, even though I am not happy in it."

4. What is the TRUTH?

....

....

....

....

....

Identifying Your Projections

A projection is a disowned and unrecognized characteristic within ourselves that we attach to someone else. When we refuse to recognize a particular characteristic or behavior in ourselves, life will present us with a person who embodies that characteristic and behavior. Life is one big projection. We project our belief systems onto everything and everyone. We are what we have been taught, some of our teachers were empowering and others disabling.

"We must recognize our projections before we can change our negative thoughts and beliefs. Like cobwebs hiding in the attic – you don't know they are there until you go up and look. As cobwebs will take over the attic if not cleaned out, so our negative thoughts and beliefs will take over our lives and make us miserable if we don't reframe them."

1. What are you projecting onto or into your life? *Example: I was abandoned as a child so I would cling to the person in my life to the point of suffocation. They couldn't take it anymore and they left.*

....

....

....

....

....

....

....

2. Where did you learn your projections? *Example: When I was young I learned that people leave. I believed that my mother did not want me; therefore I was not good enough. My feelings of being unworthy played out onto the person I was dating.*

....

....

....

....

....

....

....

....

....

....

....

....

....

....

....

....

....

....

....

....

....

3. What behavior mirrored your projection? What was the projection? *Example: My behavior, which was clinging out of fear that someone would not want me, they would leave me, mirrored my projection of unworthiness.*

....

....

....

....

....

....

....

....

....

....

....

....

....

....

....

....

....

....

....

....

....

....

4. What is the TRUTH? *Example: I was always worthy and my mother always loved me, she had her own issues that affected me but: she always loved me, she still does. I AM worthy and deserving of love!*

THE WISDOM TRIANGLE

This is a recap that you can always return to and remind yourself of the TRUTH of your situation. Be specific to the exercise you just completed. Just write down 1 or 2 sentences, keep it simple. If necessary remember that you are talking to your inner-child. What does he or she need to finally understand?

1. <u>The past:</u> (What happened?) *Example: I settled because I felt that (abuse, abandonment, verbal stress etc.,) was all that I could get*

....

....

....

....

....

2. <u>The here and now:</u> (What and why are you settling?) *Example: I am attracting the person who mirrors how I feel about myself, soiled. If I say something they will leave and then I will be alone, so I better not rock the boat.*

....

....

....

....

3. <u>The "TRUTH":</u> *Example: (What is the real healthy TRUTH about your situation?) I am good enough, I also love myself and if they don't want me, that's ok, because I want and love myself!*

....

....

....

Write 7 reasons why you forgive yourself.

1. I forgive myself for the misbelief that, and the truth is:

....

....

2. I forgive myself for the misbelief that, and the truth is:

....

....

3. I forgive myself for the misbelief that, and the truth is:

....

....

4. I forgive myself for the misbelief that, and the truth is:

....

....

5. I forgive myself for the misbelief that, and the truth is:

....

....

6. I forgive myself for the misbelief that, and the truth is:

....

....

7. I forgive myself for the misbelief that, and the truth is:

....

....

Now write 7 reasons why you are grateful.

1. I am grateful for, and the truth is:

....

....

2. I am grateful for, and the truth is:

....

....

3. I am grateful for, and the truth is:

....

....

4. I am grateful for, and the truth is:

....

....

5. I am grateful for, and the truth is:

....

....

6. I am grateful for, and the truth is:

....

....

7. I am grateful for, and the truth is:

....

....

"How do you listen? Do you listen with your projections, through your projection, through your ambitions, desires, fears, anxieties, through hearing only what you want to hear, only what will be satisfactory, what will gratify, what will give comfort, what will for the moment alleviate your suffering? If you listen through the screen of your desires, then you obviously listen to your own voice; you are listening to your own desires. And is there any other form of listening? Is it not important to find out how to listen not only to what is being said but to everything – to the noise in the streets, to the chatter of birds, to the noise of the tramcar, to the restless sea, to the voice of your husband, to your wife, to your friends, to the cry of a baby? Listening has importance only when on is not projecting one's own desires through which one listens. Can one put aside all these screens through which we listen, and really listen?"

~ Jiddu Krishnamurti, The Book of Life

EXERCISE 5 - PATH THREE - PLAYING OUT

Our behaviors reflect our hidden wounds asking to be healed.

~ Rochelle L. Cook MA., ChT.

If we find ourselves behaving in ways that are disturbing to us or to our surroundings, we better listen carefully. This behavior is an indication that something is wrong on a deeper level. We are unconsciously playing out our unresolved childhood traumas and wounds. Identifying our destructive behaviors, understanding and healing their root causes, will lead us on our journey toward the life we so wish for.

Playing Out is a Symptom to a Deeper Problem

1. What is the symptom? Example: If someone yells at me I become afraid, I hide and feel bad about myself and retreat into my world of silence. I think it's "all" my fault.

....

....

....

....

....

....

....

....

2. What behavior is upsetting you? Example: Being silent and running to my room.

....

....

....

....

....

....

....

....

....

....

....

....

....

....

....

....

....

....

....

....

....

....

....

3. What would you like to do instead? Example: Stand up for myself and understand that if it is not my fault I do not have to feel bad. It is not my responsibility to take on some else's issue.

4. What is the TRUTH? Example: I am not 5 years old, I am a adult and I am allowed to stand tall and strong. I am not helpless.

....

....

....

....

....

....

....

....

....

....

....

....

....

....

....

....

....

....

....

....

....

....

....

Every Upset is an Opportunity to Heal Once you understand the root causes of your trials and tribulations, you start making your way up into a more peaceful mind. The more we clear our minds of its shadow material, the more peaceful our minds will become.

"Your addictive and destructive behaviors are here to call you to change. They are the logs to be burned in the fire of your emotional healing and spiritual transformation. As you work on resolving your issues, watch those logs being burned to ashes and taken into the upper realms to be transmuted into love, peace and harmony."

1. What do you need to heal?

2. What new thought will allow you to heal?

WHY DO WE LOOK THE OTHER WAY?

It is a known fact that we will endure almost anything rather than change. Change is difficult.

1. **What are you afraid to change?**

....

....

....

....

....

2. **What would happen if you did change?**

....

....

....

....

....

CHASING LOVE

You do not need anyone in order to be whole – you are already whole. The road to a wonderful relationship starts with you.

Make yourself whole first. Expressions such as "she is my better half" romanticize an illusion, for a relationship between two "halves" is doomed to fail. When you're whole in yourself and rest in that knowing, you will no longer chase someone else to fill in the lack you feel inside.

When a therapist asked me: "What would happen if you sat in your chair and allowed someone to come to you," I thought she was speaking Chinese! Because I believed that no one would ever come to me.

1. Why are you whole? Name at least 10 things you like about yourself.

....

....

....

....

....

2. What would happen if you sat in your chair and allowed someone to come to you?

....

....

....

....

....

3. How would you feel if the right person wanted you, meaning, you did not chase or prove, they came to you because YOU are worthy and deserving just the way you are right here and now.

....

....

....

....

....

....

....

4._What's the TRUTH? Example: I no longer have to be afraid that someone will not want me, I can sit back in my chair, feel worthy and deserving and trust that I will find someone who will reflect back to me the way I feel about myself. WONDERFUL. **I AM** a good person! When you write this, write in, "details."

....
....
....
....
....

"All truths are easy to understand once they are discovered; the point is to discover them."~ Galileo Galilei

FEELINGS ARE NOT FACTS

They may seem to be, but most of the time they are just old memories imprinted on our "emotional body" that are being triggered in the present time, creating upset feelings.

1. What feelings are not facts?

....
....
....
....
....

2. Why are your feelings not facts?

....
....
....
....

3. How can you change your false beliefs, which turn into negative feeling into new healthy ones?

....

....

....

....

....

4. What are the new healthy ones?

....

....

....

....

....

5. What would your adult self say to your inner-child? Example: I am not just "good enough" – I was great! "I am great" became my new mantra.

....

....

....

....

....

WHAT IS MY BEHAVIOR TRYING TO TELL YOU?

Since negative behaviors are a symptom to a larger, deeper problem, behaviors such as overeating, gambling or lashing out can become our gates into the healing process.

What we learn in a traumatic childhood becomes our identity, until we unlearn it – until we heal it. What we learned, we can unlearn.

1. Which of your behaviors is an indication, a symptom, of your bigger problem?

....

....

....

....

....

2. What is your "crying to be healed" voice have to say? *Example: I am yelling at you because I am trying to get your attention and you are not listening.*

....

....

....

....

....

3. Where did you learn how to behave? *Example: My parents, or whom ever, used to yell and scream at each other. They were not listening to each other, they were also not listening to me. Read this again, THEY, not you!*

....

....

....

....

....

4. What do you **really** want? *Example: I want to be heard because you think I am important. When you do not listen to me I feel dismissed and that means I'm not good enough.*

....

....

5. What would happen and how would you feel, if you, **HEARD** yourself?

6. What would happen and how would you feel, if you did not need some else's approval?

THE WISDOM TRIANGLE

This is a recap that you can always return to and remind yourself of the TRUTH of your situation. Be specific to the exercise you just completed. Just write down 1 or 2 sentences, keep it simple. If necessary remember that you are talking to your inner-child. What does he or she need to finally understand?

1. <u>The past:</u> (**What happened?**) *Example: I attracted unhealthy people and then pushed away the love I "thought" they gave me.*

....

....

....

....

....

2. <u>The here and now:</u> (**What behavior was playing out or is playing out that you are understanding and letting go of?**) *Example: I still fear I will be alone because I'm not good enough to be loved. I live in fear and believe my own unhealthy storybook syndrome.*

....

....

....

....

....

3. <u>The "TRUTH":</u> *Example: What is the real healthy TRUTH about your situation?) My old storybook syndrome is not true! I have always been worthy of love by just being me. It does not matter what they think, it matters what "I think." I am a good person that anyone would be lucky to have in his or her lives! I hear you "fear" I am now ok!*

....

....

....

Write 7 reasons why you forgive yourself.

1. I forgive myself for the misbelief that, and the truth is:

....

....

2. I forgive myself for the misbelief that, and the truth is:

....

....

3. I forgive myself for the misbelief that, and the truth is:

....

....

4. I forgive myself for the misbelief that, and the truth is:

....

....

5. I forgive myself for the misbelief that, and the truth is:

....

....

6. I forgive myself for the misbelief that, and the truth is:

....

....

7. I forgive myself for the misbelief that, and the truth is:

....

....

Now write 7 reasons why you are grateful.

1. I am grateful for, and the truth is:

....

....

2. I am grateful for, and the truth is:

....

....

3. I am grateful for, and the truth is:

....

....

4. I am grateful for, and the truth is:

....

....

5. I am grateful for, and the truth is:

....

....

6. I am grateful for, and the truth is:

....

....

7. I am grateful for, and the truth is:

....

....

EXERCISE 6 - PATH FOUR - ACCEPTANCE

*Accepting that we have a problem is the most important step to positive transformation. ~ **Rochelle L. Cook MA., ChT.***

It is the most important step and the most difficult one. It is almost impossible to accept such challenging situations as bankruptcy or one's teenage child addiction to a heavy drug, or the infidelity of a spouse. It is equally difficult to accept our own inner "enemies" such as envy, rage or self-loathing. But when we find ourselves swallowed into the "Belly of the Whale" by any such ordeals, there is no other way but to accept our reality and continue our restoration without losing energy on resentment or debate.

What Happens When We Don't Accept? Acceptance is indeed tough and frightening, but without it there is no movement forward. If we do not accept our situation we lose energy! We get stuck. Our psyche and mind are busy resisting what is happening, our perception of possibilities is dimmed, and even if the "whale" will open its mouth we will miss it and remain stuck in the whale's dark belly.

"Everything can be taken from a man but one thing: the last of the human freedoms – to choose one's attitude in any given set of circumstances, to choose one's own way." And *"When we are no longer able to change a situation – we are challenged to change ourselves."* ~**Dr. Victor Frankl**

1. What is the most difficult thing in your life for you to accept?

....

....

....

....

....

....

....

....

....

2. What have you NOT been accepting?

....

....

....

....

....

....

....

....

....

....

....

....

....

What do you know in your deepest self you should CHOOSE to accept and what can you do to change the way you think and do what you know you need to do? (Choose to change the way you think, first and foremost about yourself, and let go of all the "do's" and the "don'ts" that were planted and imprinted into you.)

....

....

....

....

....

....

....

....

....

....

How would you feel if you honored your "choice?" (*Find the courage to rise above preconceived notions and ideas of what you should be*).

....

....

....

....

....

Become present and look at life through a new set of eyes. There is no need to dwell on the past once you have understood, cleared and healed it. There is no need to speculate about the future; often what is in store for us is way better than our wildest imaginations. Treasure the journey – be in the NOW – it will change your life and create a great future.

Acceptance is the Most Important Step to Recovery Once we accept our situation; the stuck, lost energy is released to our disposal. We can breathe now. It is said, "The truth shall set you free" ...

1. Now that you have accepted your truth, how do you feel? (When we finally recognize and accept that we are in the "belly of the whale," there is nothing else to do but feel the pain and accept our entire life story – as is – with its agony – and its glory – and ourselves as the heroes and heroines on a journey of transformation.) If acceptance could speak what would it say?

2. Why is your journey ok?

1. How Being Present and Acceptance Work Together? In one sentence what have you accepted? What are you present too?

....

....

....

....

....

....

....

....

....

2. Now that you are living in the here and now? What are you going to do to change your situation?

....

....

....

3. Are you ready to do this?

How to Change our Thoughts?

So we have an irrational thought like "Unless I change, I will never have another lover," or "I'll lose all my money," or "my girlfriend is going to leave me"... so what do I do? Well, don't suppress the thought, but don't engage in dialogue or negotiation with it either. What you can do is acknowledge the thought, feel the hurt it produces in you, make peace with it, then use your finger and press DELETE!

1. What thought are you going to delete? (Just because my mind is telling me this, does not mean that it is so.)

....

....

....

....

....

....

....

....

....

....

2. What is your new healthy thought? Your TRUTH! (Since the mind works in cycles and has the tendency to repeat itself, when the same thought will emerge again, and likely it will emerge again, you will repeat the process of acknowledging, feeling, making peace, deleting and replacing. The more you practice changing your thoughts on a regular basis, the easier and faster the process will become.)

....

....

....

....

....

....

....

....

....

....

3. How do you feel when you think the "TRUTH?

....

....

....

....

....

....

....

....

....

THE TURNING POINT

Acceptance is the turning point. The turning point means, first and foremost, turning inward. Turning inward does not mean turning away from the world or going into a cave. It means turning inward to "Know Thyself" as Socrates has taught us.

1. What does, "bottom out" mean to you? We face the fact that we have bottomed out and must do something about it if we want to be happy. Isn't the mere act of admitting and accepting already a change, a turning point?

....

....

....

....

....

....

....

. Write, "I am at my turning point." *Example: I am going to change...*

....

....

....

....

....

....

....

....

....

....

3. What did you discover that was hidden in your subconscious mind? (When we understand our life's story, some of which has been hidden in the subconscious mind, we become acquainted with more of our strengths, and talents too. This is how we turn toward ourselves!)

....

....

....

....

....

....

4. What are your strengths, and talents?

....

....

....

....

....

5. I love myself because I?

....

....

....

....

....

In each moment, with every unpleasant or irrational thought, we have a choice – a turning point – to go tumbling down with our thinking, or to change it and see our state of mind and life change as well.

It Matters What You Think, Not What "They" Think If something in your relationship is upsetting you, look carefully into your own mirror. That mirror, your relationship, is trying to teach you what you are suffering from. What is really upsetting you? Take your index finger and point it towards yourself, yes, yourself, not them!

1. Each time we are triggered is an opportunity to look at ourselves and inquire within why are we so upset. What is the other person doing that upsets you?

....

....

....

....

....

2. I am upset because "I." Not because of "them." Take personal responsibility, why are you upset? Remember, it matters what you think. YOU. *Example: I am upset because I allowed myself to be treated poorly. I am no longer what I have been taught, worthless, I am GREAT!*

....

....

....

....

3. If you are responsible for the way you think, the other person is responsible for they think, why do you now feel at peace?

....

....

....

....

....

What Have You Learned? Look back at your childhood carefully and ask yourself what have you learned. How did your parents interact with each other? How did your family, friends, teachers and neighbors relate to one another? Were they kind, warm and compassionate, offering a listening ear to the needy, or were they emotionally stingy, rigid, cold, competitive and short tempered? Who were your main caretakers and what did they teach you was right and wrong? Look back at the culture, religion and nation in which you grew up. What did these have to teach you about good and bad, the sacred and the sinful?

1. In the past, which ideas, beliefs and traditional values have you adopted without question?

....

....

....

....

....

2. Which ones have you examined and questioned or created out of your own inspiration?

....

....

....

....

....

3. Which do you choose to believe?

....

....

....

....

....

4. How do you feel now?

....

....

....

....

....

"Learn to distinguish between the world views and values you were indoctrinated into and obligated to live by, and your own discoveries, insights and personal choices. Practice being true to yourself!"

Taking Back Your Power What would it feel like to sit in your big comfortable chair and in your mind's eye let the object of your love come to you?

"Taking back your power means that you are no longer a victim, and you don't behave unconsciously and reactively. Instead, you are mindful and live in the awareness that your relationships are mirrors that reflect back to you who you are: what inside you is gracious and light, and what you still need to accept and to heal. So give thanks to the mirror, and in so doing you will also be giving thanks to yourself."

1. How would you feel if you sat back in your chair and let someone come to you?

....

....

....

....

....

2. How would you feel if you embraced who you are, loved yourself, know that you are worthy and deserving and that someone will love you for who you are right here and now?

....

....

....

....

....

3. What is **YOUR** truth?

....

....

....

....

....

....

....

....

....

....

....

THE WISDOM TRIANGLE

This is a recap that you can always return to and remind yourself of the TRUTH of your situation. Be specific to the exercise you just completed. Just write down 1 or 2 sentences, keep it simple. If necessary remember that you are talking to your inner-child. What does he or she need to finally understand?

1. The past: (What happened?) *Example: I learned that know one will love, I'll keep attracting people that abuse me, therefore I will keep abusing myself.*

....

....

....

....

....

2. The here and now: What do you need to accept understand and let go of? *Example: My unhealthy behavior is getting in the way of my happiness.*

....

....

....

....

3. The "TRUTH": *Example: What is the real healthy TRUTH about your situation? I accept I am not in a good situation and that is ok because I now know how to change my thoughts and get out of my feelings of doom and gloom.*

....

....

....

....

Write 7 reasons why you forgive yourself.

1. I forgive myself for the misbelief that, and the truth is:

....

....

2. I forgive myself for the misbelief that, and the truth is:

....

....

3. I forgive myself for the misbelief that, and the truth is:

....

....

4. I forgive myself for the misbelief that, and the truth is:

....

....

5. I forgive myself for the misbelief that, and the truth is:

....

....

6. I forgive myself for the misbelief that, and the truth is:

....

....

7. I forgive myself for the misbelief that, and the truth is:

....

....

Now write 7 reasons why you are grateful.

1. I am grateful for, and the truth is:

....

....

2. I am grateful for, and the truth is:

....

....

3. I am grateful for, and the truth is:

....

....

4. I am grateful for, and the truth is:

....

....

5. I am grateful for, and the truth is:

....

....

6. I am grateful for, and the truth is:

....

....

7. I am grateful for, and the truth is:

....

....

"Understanding is the first step to acceptance, and only with acceptance can there be recovery." **~ J. K. Rowling, Harry Potter and the Goblet of Fire**

"For after all, the best thing one can do when it is raining is let it rain." **~ Henry Wadsworth Longfellow**

EXERCISE 7 - PATH FIVE - INTENTION

"The breeze of grace is always blowing; set your sail to catch that breeze." ~ Ramakrishna Paramahansa

While the breeze of grace is always blowing, it is our job – our self-effort – to set our sails to catch that breeze. This is Intention. We may know our destination, we may know the conditions of the journey, but if we do not prepare, if we do not make all the inner and outer changes and adaptations and think-up all the steps and alliances, we'll never reach our goals, no matter how favorable the breeze of grace will be.

"It is important to create intentions that come from *your* needs, your heart, not intentions you are forced to make."

The Power of Intention The most essential intention you can make, and one that will enliven and empower every step you take, is the intention to love yourself and your life, always, whether the intentions you'll be setting materialize or not. "I intend to go to India this winter," "I plan to sign up for Internet dating," – those are intentions, there is no promise, no "contract," yet.

1. What do you declare to accomplish? First and foremost what do want and why do you want it!

....

....

....

....

....

2. How are you going to do this?

....

....

....

....

....

3. "*With sharp tools, the job is half complete ~ **Ernest Glock** .*" What tools do you now have that will help you with your intention? Example: Grace may present me with better opportunities and possibilities than I had originally intended. I will remain flexible and continue to love my process. I am in charge of what I think, not others.

....

....

....

....

4. How do you feel now?

....

....

....

....

GOALS, PLANS & ACTIONS STEPS

Start from the end, from the future, knowing how you will be feeling once your intentions have materialized. At the bottom line we all want to be happy!

When the sun of your own being shines brightly so will the rays of life engulf you in their effulgence.

1. Write down your goal. Where do you see yourself in one year? Then write down where you see yourself in 5 years, then 10 and 20. Use the appropriate numbers/ years that are best for you.

2. What are your plans? Number one is, change the way you think, use the tools you have learned in this book. List them one by one.

....

....

....

....

....

....

....

....

....

....

....

....

....

....

....

....

....

....

....

....

....

....

3. What are your action steps? Loving yourself through your process would be number one.

4. What matters is how these "things" make you feel. How does this process make you feel?

5. If something changes is that ok and why?

Commitment Intention is not commitment. Intention is setting the goal, the harbor of our destination. Commitment is the promise we make to others or to ourselves to reach that destination. When making a commitment take baby steps. Be mindful and do not bite off more than you can chew. Commit only to what you think you can achieve – and just a little bit more! Be gentle with yourself. Celebrate every little progress.

1. What is your commitment?

....

....

....

....

....

When Obstacles Arise Sometimes we just get too stuck. It is probably because in the past we experienced failure or shame or ridicule in the same or similar area. It is essential to stop and heal those painful memories.

2. What can you do if you are faced with an obstacle?

....

....

....

....

....

3. Why?

....

....

....

....

4. Name 3 things you can say to yourself if this happens.

....

....

....

....

....

ATTITUDE & GRATITUDE

A good attitude will bring about much to be grateful for.

"Recent scientific research shows that gratitude supports a stronger immune system, higher level of positive emotions, more joy, optimism, happiness and generosity, and that those who are grateful, feel less lonely and isolated."

"Walk as if you are kissing the Earth with your feet."
*~ **Thich Nhat Hanh, Peace Is Every Step: The Path of Mindfulness in Everyday Life***

1. Name 10 things that you have learned about your experience that you are now grateful for.

....

....

....

....

....

....

....

2. Why are you grateful?

....

3. How has gratitude changed your perspective, what has changed your attitude?

THE WISDOM TRIANGLE

This is a recap that you can always return to and remind yourself of the TRUTH of your situation. Be specific to the exercise you just completed. Just write down 1 or 2 sentences, keep it simple. If necessary remember that you are talking to your inner-child. What does he or she need to finally understand?

1. <u>The past:</u> (**What happened?**) Why did you not meet the goal or set your goal. *Example: I was told that goals were not achievable.*

....

....

....

....

....

2. <u>The here and now:</u> (**What behavior was playing out or is playing out that you are understanding and letting go of?**) *Example: I do not set goals or even think of them, I just get frustrated and wonder why I fail.*

....

....

....

....

....

3. <u>The "TRUTH":</u> *Example: (What is the real healthy TRUTH about your situation?) While remaining flexible I can set a goal and I will achieve it.*

....

....

....

....

Write 7 reasons why you forgive yourself.

1. I forgive myself for the misbelief that, and the truth is:

2. I forgive myself for the misbelief that, and the truth is:

3. I forgive myself for the misbelief that, and the truth is:

4. I forgive myself for the misbelief that, and the truth is:

5. I forgive myself for the misbelief that, and the truth is:

6. I forgive myself for the misbelief that, and the truth is:

7. I forgive myself for the misbelief that, and the truth is:

Now write 7 reasons why you are grateful.

1. I am grateful for, and the truth is:

....

....

2. I am grateful for, and the truth is:

....

....

3. I am grateful for, and the truth is:

....

....

4. I am grateful for, and the truth is:

....

....

5. I am grateful for, and the truth is:

....

....

6. I am grateful for, and the truth is:

....

....

7. I am grateful for, and the truth is:

....

....

EXERCISE 8 - PATH SIX- SPIRITUALITY

"Your Task Is Not to Seek for Love, but Merely to Seek and Find
All the Barriers Within Yourself That You Have Built Against It."
~ Rumi

"The wound is the place where the Light enters you.
~ Rumi

Spirituality is both a point of view and a practice. It is the understanding that we come to this life with a purpose, and the purpose is to live in the Loving that is our basic nature. Everything we have experienced since childhood to the present day has created who we are today. The lessons we've learned amplify our wisdom and strength, our positive attitude, and our grateful hearts. We no longer point the finger; we no longer live in a "house of glass and throw stones." We have become more whole. Meditation, contemplation, chanting, art, walks in nature, are tools that help us sustain our wellbeing and bring us back to center when we fall off.

SPIRITUALITY AND MINDFULNESS

Spirituality may refer to any kind of meaningful activity that evokes and supports a peaceful, focused state of mind in which we are fully present in the here and now. Being mindful, living in the here and now, is the experience of an actress performing on stage, a mother nursing her baby, or anyone absorbed by a sunset or the playfulness of dolphins in the sea.

1. What does spirituality and mindfulness mean to you?

....

....

....

....

....

2. What are you doing to become more mindful?

....

....

....

....

....

3. How does your practice make you feel?

....

....

....

....

....

The Soul and the Human Experience A soul comes into this world with a purpose. Since life on this planet is a school, with a curriculum, and since suffering is innate to our world as we know it, this purpose will be met by obstacles

*"The new spirituality is that it will produce an experience in human encounters in which we become a living demonstration of the basic spiritual teaching 'We are all one." ~ **Neale Donald Walsch***

*"The wound is the place where the Light enters you." ~ **Rumi***

1. What have you learned about your experience? What are your lessons? Example: I have LEARNED how to better have compassion for others as well as myself. I am not what I experienced; I am what I have become, strong, loving and courageous. **I am love.** I am not weak and not worthy, I am not damaged goods. The lessons I have learned have only made me stronger so that I can stand on my own two feet. I can now hold the light not only for myself, but others.

....

....

....

....

....

2. Name a few lessons that you have learned. Example: compassion, strength, my parents were doing at the time the best they could. We all are. We all have our curriculum to face.

....

....

....

....

....

3. How are you able to help others? Turning our wounds into compassion and becoming the healers and helpers of our world let us feel that we have not suffered in vain.

....

....

....

....

....

The Book of Wisdom. Our stories – the glorious and the miserable ones – make up the tapestry of our lives. Embrace all your experiences for they are the chapters in your book of wisdom.

1. What are the most important chapters in your life?

....

....

....

....

2. Why?

....

....

....

....

....

3. How have you made peace with them and let them go?

....

....

....

....

....

4. Why are you now proud of yourself? Acknowledge yourself.

....

....

....

....

"Make your own Bible. Select and collect all the words and sentences that in all your readings have been to you like the blast of a trumpet." Ralph Waldo Emerson

What does "Meaning" mean? Think for a moment how frustrated you can become when you don't understand a foreign language spoken around you, or the plot twist in a film or book, or the unexpected behavior of a friend. Now remember the ah-ha – the relief – you feel when things are explained. The mind loves to understand.

Through recovery, we reclaim our soul and find a new meaningful life.

*"Ultimately, man should not ask what the meaning of his life is, but rather he must recognize that it is he who is asked." ~ **Viktor E. Frankl***

1. What is the meaning behind your experience? Assign meaning to facts and events in your life that will shed light on some of your questions. Example: The meaning of my experience showed me my path to walk. I can now with empathy and understanding help others find the light at the end of the tunnel.

....

....

....

....

....

2. You may not want to repeat your experience however; what are you grateful for? List several reasons.

....

....

....

....

....

3. Do you hold more wisdom then before? Example: I am no longer judging another persons experience; their curriculum belongs to them. I will only hold another living being compassion and light.

....

....

....

....

....

Forgiveness When practicing forgiveness it is important to forgive yourself and the other person. Forgiveness does not mean that one's worthiness is contingent upon your holly, God like "I forgive you" statement. You are forgiving because you recognize that "you" are forgiving the soul having a human experience.

*"The weak can never forgive. Forgiveness is the attribute of the strong. ~ **Mahatma Gandhi**"*

1. What are you forgiving yourself for? Example: I forgive myself for believing that I was never good enough. The **TRUTH** is that I have always been so. Please write at least 10.

....

....

....

....

....

2. Who are you forgiving beside yourself? Why? For what? Name at least 10. Take your time with this, it is important!

....

....

....

....

3. Why are you practicing forgiveness?

4. How do you feel now?

THE WISDOM TRIANGLE

This is a recap that you can always return to and remind yourself of the TRUTH of your situation. Be specific to the exercise you just completed. Just write down 1 or 2 sentences, keep it simple. If necessary remember that you are talking to your inner-child. What does he or she need to finally understand?

1. The past: (What happened?) *Example: I attracted people into my life, that mirrored how I felt about myself. Thank you Spirit I am becoming a better person.*

....

....

....

....

....

2. The here and now: (What are you learning?) *Example: Upset is only an opportunity to learn and grow. My past and what I was taught does not define who I am now.*

....

....

....

....

....

3. The "TRUTH": Example: (What is the real healthy TRUTH about your situation?)
The lessons I have learned have taught me to become a better person.

....

....

....

....

Write 7 reasons why you forgive yourself.

1. I forgive myself for the misbelief that, and the truth is:

....

....

2. I forgive myself for the misbelief that, and the truth is:

....

....

3. I forgive myself for the misbelief that, and the truth is:

....

....

4. I forgive myself for the misbelief that, and the truth is:

....

....

5. I forgive myself for the misbelief that, and the truth is:

....

....

6. I forgive myself for the misbelief that, and the truth is:

....

....

7. I forgive myself for the misbelief that, and the truth is:

....

....

Now write 7 reasons why you are grateful.

1. I am grateful for, and the truth is:

....

....

2. I am grateful for, and the truth is:

....

....

3. I am grateful for, and the truth is:

....

....

4. I am grateful for, and the truth is:

....

....

5. I am grateful for, and the truth is:

....

....

6. I am grateful for, and the truth is:

....

....

7. I am grateful for, and the truth is:

....

....

"Enlightened leadership is spiritual if we understand spirituality not as some kind of religious dogma or ideology but as the domain of awareness where we experience values like truth, goodness, beauty, love and compassion, and also intuition, creativity, insight and focused attention." ~ **Deepak Chopra**

EXERCISE 9 - PATH SEVEN - THE NEW STORY

"Free Yourself From the Endless Slavery of Your Old Story; You Get to Choose Who You Wish to Become."

~ Rochelle L. Cook MA., ChT.

Our old story has set us up for much pain and failure. It wasn't really "our story," but we came to believe it was due to past conditioning and trauma. The new story sets us up for joy and success in all areas. It's a rewrite: from a victim's experience of life to living in the awareness that our true essence is Loving and that we are the cocreator of our lives – of our new story – a heroic story as such!

SAYING GOODBYE TO THE PAST FOR THE LAST TIME

Having refused the "Call to Action" – the call to healing and transformation as elucidated in the Hero's Journey – and opted instead to deny, settle and play out your subconscious harmful story. NOW as difficult as it was to admit it, you set out on the paths of Intention and Spirituality to confront your deepest fears and demons. You understood the forces that had caused your trauma, you uncovered where your root issues had stemmed from, and you have healed, and forgiven. What a journey it has been! It's now time to bring back the boon you have been granted – bring it back to yourself! Joseph Campbell calls this stage on the Hero's Journey, "The Return with the Boon" this means the return to your authentic story, the one you were meant to live, the one where all your talents and natural gifts flourish and your dreams bloom.

WRITING YOUR NEW STORY

Sustenance means re-writing your life story and then keeping it updated every day – not on paper, but in mind, heart and deed.

The 4-Part Process to Rewriting Your Story (Please feel free to write as much as you need to finally **let go**. If you decide to burn what you have written, allow the Great Spirit to take away your old story, please do so safely.)

1. **What Was the Situation or Incident?** (This part #1 is to be burned. Write it here first as a rehearsal then on a separate piece of paper.) Example: My issue was around abandonment. Because of my childhood I grew up feeling not good enough for love. As an adult I played out the destructive behaviors I learned as a child and they ruled my life causing me much devastation. (Use loose leaf paper because you are going to burn it.)

....

....

....

....

....

2. **How did it affect You?** (Part #2 is to be burned) Example: The effects were devastating. In the absence of a mother's attention and trust in her love for me, I grew up to become a woman who chased love wherever I could find it. When I was denied, I felt as though a death took place and I was unable to cope. (Use loose leaf paper because you are going to burn it.)

....

....

....

....

....

....

....

....

....

The New Story (Do not burn!) None of it was true. My mother always wanted me and adored me! She just had too many problems of her own to be able to mother me properly. (This is an important step so please take your time. See chapter 10) (You may need extra paper for this assignment).

....

....

....

....

....

Look at your life as a prayer, your deeds and words the themes in the new story you are writing, and you will become what you write.

1. **Letters to the Person, or Persons, who Hurt You, and/or a letter to Yourself** (Don't burn!) Write a letter of love and forgiveness to the person or persons who hurt you the most. You can also write a letter to yourself and heal the most important relationship – the one to oneself. (KEEP WRITING AND TAKE YOUR TIME.) (You may need extra paper for this assignment). You do not need to show this letter to anyone.

....

....

....

....

....

....

....

....

....

....

2. This is an important step take your time. Write to everyone you have named in this workbook. (Here are some examples) Use the lined pages coming up, you can also use your journal). (You may need extra paper for this assignment). You do not need to show this letter to anyone.

....

....

....

....

....

....

....

....

"There's so much grey to every story - nothing is so black and white." ~ Lisa Ling

Dear Mom,

Thank you Mommy for all the lessons you have taught me. You are so wise. You helped me travel up the learning line of life. You have always been my teacher. You have always told me that I would never be alone and that God/Spirit is by my side. As a child I remember you reading me two beautiful poems I shall never forget, Footprints in the Sand - by Mary Stevenson, and Desiderata - by Max Ehrmann.

As a child you loved and cherished me. You'd brush my hair and dress me up like a little princess. I know that in your eyes I was the meaning of life. I always knew that no matter what, I could come to you for help, love and wisdom. No matter what, you would always be here for me. You still are. Your own problems had nothing to do with me. As you said many times, "If my death could take all that I have done to you, I would let it." You did nothing "to" me. Life's circumstances had a plan for both of us. Our experiences have taught us how to be kind, non-judgmental and compassionate towards others. This of course includes ourselves.

I forgive myself for buying into the misbelief that I was not loved and that you did not want me. The truth is you always did, life was just challenging for you, which made things difficult.

I have learned that perceptions need questioning. By keeping an open mind and letting go of my own judgments and misbeliefs, I have healed my childhood wounds; they have been but stepping stones to make me who I have become. Thank you.

I want to tell you how much you mean to me!

I admire you and the journey you have traveled. I thank you for your wisdom and your appreciation for who I have become. I thank you for everything you have done, who you were and who you are today. Thank you for teaching me to believe in myself. And for wonderful gems of advise, like: "Those who live in glass houses should not throw stones," and "we can run but we cannot hide, wherever we go, there we will be."

I love you,
Rochelle

Dearest Rochelle,

You have come such a long way. Your strength and courage have blossomed your soul. You are no longer living your life in fear for you have found your ancient roots. Your ancestors have always been behind you, supporting and guiding you on your life's lessons. Be quiet and still, listen to the whisper of their words. Your tree of life has always sheltered you from the cold. Be grateful for your experiences, for they have given you the wisdom to see the true meaning of life. Such a gift the heavens have bestowed upon you!

Rochelle, you are not alone, you never will be. I will always be here by your side. I will always hold your hand. As you walk down the river of life remember to bless the currents you encounter. As you continue to travel down your beautiful journey remember to "swim down the stream."

Be as you are, love all that is around you, see what is before you, and without judgment accept what you cannot change. As you walk, listen, and fully embrace the wisdom that guides you through your travels.

Rochelle, the greatest gift you can give to others is to love yourself.

With love,
Rochelle

THE WISDOM TRIANGLE

This is a recap that you can always return to and remind yourself of the TRUTH of your situation. Be specific to the exercise you just completed. Just write down 1 or 2 sentences, keep it simple. If necessary remember that you are talking to your inner-child. What does he or she need to finally understand?

1. <u>The past:</u> (What happened?) *Example: I had to walk a difficult journey so I could become who I am today. Read the conclusion in the book – **The Soul's Coach – 7 Paths to Healing Your Relationship** From Grapes to Vinegar.*

....

....

....

....

2. <u>The here and now:</u> (What behavior was playing out or is playing out that you are understanding and letting go of?) *Example: I am grateful that I have gained a new understanding so that I can now walk down a path of peace.*

....

....

....

....

3. <u>The "TRUTH":</u> (What is the real healthy TRUTH about your situation?) *Example: I was summoned to experience trauma so that I could become the teacher I am today.*

....

....

....

Write 7 reasons why you forgive yourself.

1. I forgive myself for the misbelief that, and the truth is:

2. I forgive myself for the misbelief that, and the truth is:

3. I forgive myself for the misbelief that, and the truth is:

4. I forgive myself for the misbelief that, and the truth is:

5. I forgive myself for the misbelief that, and the truth is:

6. I forgive myself for the misbelief that, and the truth is:

7. I forgive myself for the misbelief that, and the truth is:

Now write 7 reasons why you are grateful.

1. I am grateful for, and the truth is:

....

....

2. I am grateful for, and the truth is:

....

....

3. I am grateful for, and the truth is:

....

....

4. I am grateful for, and the truth is:

....

....

5. I am grateful for, and the truth is:

....

....

6. I am grateful for, and the truth is:

....

....

7. I am grateful for, and the truth is:

....

....

EXERCISE 10 - REFLECTIONS ON PARENTING

(For those of you that have children or are thinking about children)

Each day of our lives we make deposits in the memory banks or
our children." ~ Charles R. Swindoll

When it comes to children, we, as adults, must pay attention to our words and behavior. Many adults suffered trauma in childhood and it's running their lives to this day. It is important for adults to understand and heal their own life's suffering, so as not to project their "agenda" onto their children. If a parent experienced abuse in her/or his childhood, the parent now is likely to abuse their child. The child will grow up believing and expecting such abuse, and if not healed, the pattern will continue into the next generations. Our children are the future of the world and our most precious asset.

"Children must be taught how to think, not what to think." ~ Margaret Mead, cultural anthropologist

Children Don't Talk Favorable as well as dysfunctional ancestral family patterns are transported from generation to generation. In the case of the latter, in order to stop the dysfunction from perpetuating, it must rise up in the awareness of a family member down the line who will heal it.

To support your child in having a happy healthy life, heal your own trauma, lest you risk transmitting it on. Unless your issues are made conscious and your sorrows healed, you will pass them to your descendants.

1. When is the last time you asked your child to tell you about their lives and how they feel?

....

....

....

....

....

2. If you watch your child's actions what are they doing?

....

....

....

....

....

3. Is your child mirroring an unhealthy reflection of someone around you? Maybe you? *Example: Screaming, fighting, sadness, fear, withdrawal etc.*

....

....

....

....

4. What are their actions trying to tell you? Are they afraid to sleep alone? Do they not want to go to school? Why? Are you afraid of something?

....

....

....

....

5. Do you feel that you can help them or do they need a professional? Maybe your child/
children are perfectly fine which would be great.

....

....

....

....

....

Boys Don't Cry and Obsessive Perfectionism Many clients have walked into my office expressing fear that they would be abandoned or punished for having done something wrong.

1. Does your child think that they cannot cry or show any type of weakness?

....

....

....

....

....

2. Do they have to be perfect to win your approval?

....

....

....

....

....

....

3. Did you or do you do the same thing?

....

....

....

....

....

4. Where did you or your child learn this?

....

....

....

....

....

5. How can you change the way you and or your child think?

....

....

....

....

6. What is the truth?

....

....

....

....

....

*"There can be no keener revelation of a society's soul than the way in which it treats its children." ~ **Nelson Mandela, Former President of South Africa***

It's Not the Child's Job to Take Care of the Parent – Children Don't Talk

A well-known phenomenon predicates that children accept and forgive what they see in their homes; they need their parents so they accept the good with the bad.

"This is what I learned from my daughter: I learned that when children become even slightly illusive, it means that they are hiding something. Children feel, but they don't know how to describe what they feel so they react: some become angry and sad, others become shy and withdrawn. It is their subconscious cry for help, the only way they know how. "

1. Think carefully, is your child trying to ask you something? Look at their behavior. If you suspect something you may consider **seeing a professional for help**. Some examples **may** be; the child does not want to go to school because they feel scared or inadequate, why? Do they have trouble socializing with others? Are they afraid for some reason to leave home? Are they afraid to sleep alone? Do they think it's their fault that Mommy and Daddy got a divorce? The list is unfortunately endless. It is time for you and/or the professional to figure this out.

2. Have you tried to be creative with your child and ask what's happening in **their lives?** Draw pictures; ask questions like; can you draw me a picture of what school looks like or what happens in school, whatever you, the adult, think may be the problem. Say nothing; just sit down with your child and color. When children are young they do not know how to express themselves verbally.

....

....

3. When is the last time you checked in with the teachers or other people around your child?

....

....

....

....

....

4. How do they treat their toys, siblings, you and their friends? Pay attention. What do you see? What are you hearing?

....

....

....

....

....

5. Please, take the time to play with your child. Bravo to those of you who do. What are 5 things you can do with your child? What do **THEY** want to do? They not you.

....

....

....

....

....

You cannot love a child too much, but don't suffocate the child with too much love either. Children need to be nurtured and cultivated like a plant or a garden or a work of art. In fact they are your highest and finest works of art! They need to be acknowledged for their talents and strengths, supported in their weaker areas, and always told how wonderful they are. If you can't do that, you probably have not healed your own emotional wounds and are most likely projecting them onto your child.

Parental love is the foundation for being secure, self-confident and successful in adulthood.

Teach your child to keep a good attitude and self-love, especially when life presents challenges and obstacles.

1. How are you nurturing your child?

....

....

....

....

....

2. What about you that YOU love about yourself, including your wisdom, are you passing onto your child?

....

....

....

....

....

3. As of now, what is your child's talents and strengths? Do not judge, look at **them** only. More will unfold later in their life, people change and that is ok. Look at the now.

....

....

....

....

....

4. How can you acknowledged your child? It is important to acknowledge and prize them at the level they are at now. A 4 year old will not understand the same thing as a 30 year old.

....

....

....

....

....

5. How can you LOVINGLY and in a POSITIVE way support your child's weaker areas? Remember to make what ever they are struggling with ok. We all have our issues and **nothing is wrong,** it's just that we were all not meant to be the president of the United States, or India, or Brazil or New Zealand!

....

....

....

....

....

6. What do you wish YOU had been more supportive in, in your child lifetime?

....

....

....

....

....

7. Did someone project his or her beliefs onto you meaning, what would you have liked?

....

....

....

....

....

"Children are likely to live up to what you believe of them." ~ Lady Bird Johnson, Former First Lady of the United States

8. Are you doing this to your child?

....

....

....

....

....

....

....

Letters to Santa When my daughter was young, one of the ways in which she expressed her feelings was to write in her pink sparkled journal. She wrote letters to Santa Clause. I believe that writing in her journal, she was speaking to the Great Spirit. When she wrote to Santa she was talking to someone she believed would help her. She trusted in magic.

It is important for children to have outlets to express their feelings, both joyful and troubling. Help your children find creative ways to channel their energies.

1. Did your inner-child write a letter to someone?

....

....

....

....

....

2. When is the last time your own child wrote a letter to his or her hero?

....

....

....

....

....

3. Can you in a playful non- direct way influence your child to write so someone or draw a picture?

....

....

....

....

....

....

....

....

....

....

THE WISDOM TRIANGLE

This is a recap that you can always return to and remind yourself of the TRUTH of your situation. Be specific to the exercise you just completed. Just write down 1 or 2 sentences, keep it simple. If necessary remember that you are talking to your inner-child. What does he or she need to finally understand?

1. <u>The past:</u> (What happened?) *Example: What has your child's actions tried to tell you?*

....

....

....

....

....

2. The here and now: What behavior of your child is playing out what are they trying to communicate? Please listen to their words and observe their actions.

....

....

....

....

3. <u>The "TRUTH"</u>: How can you take personal responsibility for your thoughts and actions that have influenced your child or is something else happening in school or with friends etc.

....

....

....

....

Write 7 reasons why you forgive yourself. *BE AS SPECIFIC AS YOU CAN.*

1. I forgive myself for the misbelief that, and the truth is:

....

....

2. I forgive myself for the misbelief that, and the truth is:

....

....

3. I forgive myself for the misbelief that, and the truth is:

....

....

4. I forgive myself for the misbelief that, and the truth is:

....

....

5. I forgive myself for the misbelief that, and the truth is:

....

....

6. I forgive myself for the misbelief that, and the truth is:

....

....

7. I forgive myself for the misbelief that, and the truth is:

....

....

Now write 7 reasons why you are grateful.

1. I am grateful for, and the truth is:

....

....

2. I am grateful for, and the truth is:

....

....

3. I am grateful for, and the truth is:

....

....

4. I am grateful for, and the truth is:

....

....

5. I am grateful for, and the truth is:

....

....

6. I am grateful for, and the truth is:

....

....

7. I am grateful for, and the truth is:

....

"Words, especially when yelled in anger, can be very damaging to a child's self-confidence. The child probably already feels bad enough just from seeing the consequences of his or her behavior. Our sons and daughters don't need more guilt and self-doubt heaped upon their already wounded egos." ~ **Jack Canfield**

EXERCISE 11 - REFLECTIONS

Conclusion *Accept and Honor All Your Past Experiences, Good and Bad, so You Can Flavor the Palette of Your Own Life.*

1. What have you concluded from participating in this workbook?

....

....

....

....

....

....

....

....

....

2. In the book, *The Soul's Coach – 7 Paths to Healing Your Relationship*, a story had been written. Using the story in the book as an example, what is your NEW STORY? Keep it all positive! An example can be found in chapter 12.

....

....

....

....

THE WISDOM TRIANGLE

This is a recap that you can always return to and remind yourself of the TRUTH of your situation. Be specific to the exercise you just completed. Just write down 1 or 2 sentences, keep it simple. If necessary remember that you are talking to your inner-child. What does he or she need to finally understand?

1. The past: (What happened?) *Example: Write from a spiritual perspective.*

....

....

....

....

....

2. The here and now: *Example: Write from a spiritual perspective.*

....

....

....

....

....

....

....

3. The "TRUTH": *Example: Write from a spiritual perspective.*

....

....

....

....

Write 7 reasons why you forgive yourself. BE AS SPECIFIC AS YOU CAN.

1. I forgive myself for the misbelief that, and the truth is:

2. I forgive myself for the misbelief that, and the truth is:

3. I forgive myself for the misbelief that, and the truth is:

4. I forgive myself for the misbelief that, and the truth is:

5. I forgive myself for the misbelief that, and the truth is:

6. I forgive myself for the misbelief that, and the truth is:

7. I forgive myself for the misbelief that, and the truth is:

Now write 7 reasons why you are grateful.

1. I am grateful for, and the truth is:

....

....

2. I am grateful for, and the truth is:

....

....

3. I am grateful for, and the truth is:

....

....

4. I am grateful for, and the truth is:

....

....

5. I am grateful for, and the truth is:

....

....

6. I am grateful for, and the truth is:

....

....

7. I am grateful for, and the truth is:

....

....

Now, I believe that everyone has a, "proof board," This means that you can write down 10 things or more if you choose to look at when ever you need some extra support. What 10 things have you done that you can feel good about? Name 10 things that allow you to pat yourself on your back. I can think of one right now,

You were born and are living the curriculum
that you were summoned to experience.

You have completed this workbook, now keep going! Some people write that they have been able to create a successful job or that they are now a parent who loves their child. In my office I ask my clients to write a 100 of these! Yes, it takes time but you will turn your thinking around and really learn to love yourself in the process. Feel free to do this with someone you may not like. We can all change our thoughts and beliefs. All we have to do is let go of the judgments of others, and ourselves and we will set ourselves free. Remember; this work that you have done is a practice, a new way of thinking, a new way of life. Stay focused and committed to the practice and you will see results. It takes time but taking one step at a time will build the new healthy muscle that will keep you balanced. Happy writing!

TAKE THE CHALLENGE: NAME 100 THINGS THAT YOU LIKE ABOUT YOURSELF. YOU CAN DO IT!

1. ....
2. ....
3. ....
4. ....
5. ....
6. ....
7. ....
8. ....
9. ....
10. ....
11. ....
12. ....
13. ....
14. ....
15. ....
16. ....
17. ....
18. ....
19. ....
20. ....
21. ....
22. ....
23. ....
24. ....

25. ....

26. ....

27. ....

28. ....

29. ....

30. ....

31. ....

32. ....

33. ....

34. ....

35. ....

36. ....

37. ....

38. ....

39. ....

40. ....

41. ....

42. ....

43. ....

44. ....

45. ....

46. ....

47. ....

48. ....

49. ....

50. ....

51. ....

52. ....

53. ....

54. ....

55. ....

56. ....

57. ....

58. ....

59. ....

60. ....

61. ....

62. ....

63. ....

64. ....

65. ....

66. ....

67. ....

68. ....

69. ....

70. ....

71. ....

72. ....

73. ....

74. ....

75. ....

76. ....

77. ....

78. ....

79. ....

80. ....

81. ....

82. ....

83. ....

84. ....

85. ....

86. ....

87. ....

88. ....

89. ....

90. ....

91. ....

92. ....

93. ....

94. ....

95. ....

96. ....

97. ....

98. ....

99. ....

100. ....

A Tree Says: My Strength is Trust

For me, trees have always been the most penetrating preachers. I revere them when they live in tribes and families, in forests and groves. And even more I revere them when they stand-alone. They are like lonely persons. Not like hermits who have stolen away out of some weakness, but like great, solitary men, like Beethoven and Nietzsche. In their highest boughs the world rustles, their roots rest in infinity; but they do not lose themselves there, they struggle with all the force of their lives for one thing only: to fulfill themselves according to their own laws, to build up their own form, to represent themselves. Nothing is holier; nothing is more exemplary than a beautiful, strong tree. When a tree is cut down and reveals its naked death-wound to the sun, one can read its whole history in the luminous, inscribed disk of its trunk: in the rings of its years, its scars, all the struggle, all the suffering, all the sickness, all the happiness and prosperity stand truly written, the narrow years and the luxurious years, the attacks withstood, the storms endured. And every young farm boy knows that the hardest and noblest wood has the narrowest rings, that high on the mountains and in continuing danger the most indestructible, the strongest, the ideal trees grow.

Trees are sanctuaries. Whoever knows how to speak to them, whoever knows how to listen to them, can learn the truth. They do not preach learning and precepts, they preach, undeterred by particulars, the ancient law of life.

A tree says: A kernel is hidden in me, a spark, a thought; I am life from eternal life. The attempt and the risk that the eternal mother took with me is unique, as unique as the form and veins of my skin, unique as the smallest play of leaves in my branches and the smallest scar on my bark. I was made to form and reveal the eternal in my smallest special detail.

A tree says: My strength is trust. I know nothing about my fathers; I know nothing about the thousand children that every year spring out of me. I live out the secret of my seed to the very end, and I care for nothing else. I trust that God is in me. I trust that my labor is holy. Out of this trust I live.

When we are stricken and cannot bear our lives any longer, then a tree has something to say to us: Be still! Be still! Look at me! Life is not easy, life is not difficult. Those are childish thoughts. Let God speak within you, and your thoughts will grow silent. You are anxious because your path leads away from mother and home. But every step and every day lead you back again to the mother. Home is neither here nor there. Home is within you, or home is nowhere at all.

A longing to wander tears my heart when I hear trees rustling in the wind at evening. If one listens to them silently for a long time, this longing reveals its kernel, its meaning. It is not so much a matter of escaping from one's suffering, though it may seem to be so. It is a longing for home, for a memory of the mother, for new metaphors for life. It leads home. Every path leads homeward, every step is birth, every step is death, every grave is mother.

So the tree rustles in the evening, when we stand uneasy before our own childish thoughts: Trees have long thoughts, long-breathing and restful, just as they have longer lives than ours. They are wiser than we are, as long as we do not listen to them. But when we have learned how to listen to trees, then the brevity and the quickness and the childlike hastiness of our thoughts achieve an incomparable joy. Whoever has learned how to listen to trees no longer wants to be a tree. He wants to be nothing except what he is. That is home. That is happiness."

~ Hermann Hesse, Bäume. Betrachtungen und Gedichte

CONNECT

With Rochelle L. Cook MA., ChT.

Since 2008, Rochelle L. Cook has introduced The Soul's Coaching Programs to thousands of people throughout the world. Visit her **online and become a member of the tribe** www. TheSoulsCoach.com

♦ Learn more about The Soul's Coaching Programs

♦ Become a member and listen and watch audio and video clips of Rochelle speaking and coaching. Connect with others on the forum, take online courses: www. TheSoulsCoach.com

♦ Find out about weekend and scheduled workshop retreats

♦ Schedule a session with Rochelle: Book online www.RochelleLCook.com

♦ Visit Rochelle on Facebook: rochelle.cook.587

♦ Visit Rochelle on LinkedIn: www.linkedin.com/in/thesoulscoach

♦ Visit Rochelle on Twitter: rochellelcook

♦ Visit Rochelle on Google+: https://plus.google.com/+RochelleLCook/

♦ Visit Rochelle: www.RochelleLCook.com

Change and shifts will always be a part of your life. Follow me and become a member of our growing tribe.

Nameste

Notes

CONNECT

With Rochelle L. Cook MA., ChT.

Since 2008, Rochelle L. Cook has introduced The Soul's Coaching Programs to thousands of people throughout the world. Visit her **online and become a member of the tribe** www. thesoulscoach.com

- ◆ Learn more about The Soul's Coaching Programs

- ◆ Become a member and listen and watch audio and video clips of Rochelle speaking and coaching

- ◆ Find out about weekend and scheduled workshop retreats

- ◆ Schedule a session with Rochelle

- ◆ Visit Rochelle on Facebook: rochelle.cook.587

- ◆ Visit Rochelle on LinkedIn: www.linkedin.com/in/thesoulscoach

- ◆ Visit Rochelle on Twitter: rochellelcook

- ◆ Visit Rochelle on Google+: https://plus.google.com/+RochelleLCook/

- ◆ Visit Rochelle on the Blog: www.thesoulscoach.com

- ◆ Visit Rochelle at www.RochelleLCook.com

Change and shifts will always be a part of your life. Follow me and become a member of our growing tribe.

Nameste

www.ingramcontent.com/pod-product-compliance
Lightning Source LLC
LaVergne TN
LVHW061300060426

835509LV00016B/1651

9 780989 193139